LOST LINES OF WALES
CAMBRIAN COAST LINE

TOM FERRIS

GRAFFEG

CONTENTS

FOREWORD

This series of books aims to revive nostalgic memories of some of the more interesting and scenic railways that served the people of Wales and visitors to the country.

This volume, unlike its siblings, is about a line that is still very much in existence, though greatly changed from its glory days. The sublimely beautiful Great Western Railway steam locomotives and the line's very own named train, the *Cambrian Coast Express*, which they hauled, are only memories now. But you can still turn up at any railway station in Britain and buy a ticket enabling you to savour the scenic majesty of the Cambrian Coast Line from the comfort, if that is not an oxymoron, of an ageing diesel railcar.

This line is a survivor. Though it was not one of the many threatened with closure in the infamous Beeching Report of the 1960s, the routes feeding traffic onto it at Barmouth Junction/Morfa Mawddach and Afon Wen were closed in that decade. Closure of the coast line was proposed in the 1970s but it survived, though it lost its goods services; stations became unstaffed and signaling was rationalised, reducing its capacity. It survived these traditional threats to the country railway to be almost felled by a tiny marine worm. This was discovered in the 1980s boring into and weakening the wooden pillars supporting the line's major engineering feature, the lengthy bridge over the estuary at Barmouth. Fortunately British Rail repaired the bridge and the danger of closure was again averted. Today it carries a healthy level of traffic especially during the summer months. Through trains to Pwllheli were suspended for nine months in 2014 following problems with another bridge. This time it was the replacement of Pont Briwet, which took the railway and a road over the River Dwyryd near Penrhyndeudraeth, that caused the problem. Even though there was length disruption for passengers, closure was never on the agenda – perhaps a sign that, in this respect at least, we live in more enlightened times.

INTRODUCTION

Few would deny that one of the most picturesque stretches of railway line open in Britain today is that which runs from Dovey Junction along the shores of Cardigan Bay to Pwllheli. It never strays far from the coast and from the windows of its trains a constantly changing panorama of sand and water is a delight to the traveller. That it has survived a century and a half of battering from the adjacent sea is a tribute to those who built it. Its endurance against more recent threats, ranging from the anti-railway sentiments which prevailed in government in the 1960s and the unlikely, but potentially destructive, attention its main engineering feature, the Barmouth Bridge, suffered from a species of wood-loving marine worm in the 1980s, is perhaps down to good fortune.Given the carnage inflicted on the railways of Wales in the 1960s, that good fortune is more than deserved.

Attempts to build railways across mid Wales dated back to the 1830s. At that time many railway promoters myopically focused on grand trunk lines to ports in north Wales from whence the Irish mails could be sped to London. A favoured destination for such schemes was Porth Dinllaen on the Lleyn Peninsula. Both C. B. Vignoles and I. K. Brunel surveyed lines to Porth Dinllaen, the latter's would have included a tunnel under Cader Idris to reach the coast. Wiser counsels prevailed in the 1840s when George Stephenson surveyed the relatively flat strip along the north Wales coast from Chester to Holyhead which became the route of the Irish mails from 1848. Despite attempts to extend the line, which was eventually built from Pwllheli across the Lleyn Peninsula as late as the early twentieth century, Porth Dinllaen was destined never to echo to the whistles of steam locomotives.

The failure of those early schemes was perhaps coupled to a realisation that if the Irish traffic was no longer up for grabs, there was limited potential to make money by driving railways through thinly populated and largely rural areas of mid Wales. This led to a long hiatus in attempts to bring railways to the area and it was not until the 1850s that something actually happened on the ground. The first line to be opened was in 1859, the isolated Llanidloes & Newtown built by the great David Davies, Wales' very own member of that pantheon of larger than life Victorian engineers and industrialists who changed the face of Britain. The L&N was connected to the Oswestry & Newtown in 1861 which in turn linked up to the Shrewsbury & Welshpool in 1865. A route through Mid Wales to the coast was being developed in a piecemeal fashion and was extended over the fearsome Talerddig summit by the Newtown & Machynlleth line which opened in 1863. Just before this, in 1861, the Aberystwyth & Welch Coast Railway entered the fray and received parliamentary approval for its line from Aberystwyth to Pwllheli. The original intention of the company was to bridge the Dovey at Ynyslas from where, at low tide, Aberdovey on the other shore seems invitingly close. However, it was impossible to find secure foundations for a bridge here so the line was extended along the shores

of the estuary towards Machynlleth. It opened between Machynlleth and Borth on 1st July 1863 and trains began running on the remaining 8¾ miles to Aberystwyth in June 1864.

Once Aberystwyth was connected to Machynlleth momentum slowed. This was partly due to a lack of funds, an issue which plagued the building of many lines in the more rural parts of Wales. The first section of the coast line to be built, the relatively level and straightforward stretch from Aberdovey to Llwyngwril, was opened in isolation in October 1864 along with a branch to Aberdovey Harbour. Hopes that Aberdovey would develop as a significant port were never realised. Engines and rolling stock to work the new railway had to be brought in by sea, though one wonders how much traffic this line going, in truth, nowhere would have generated. With the abandonment of the plan for a bridge across the Dovey estuary at Ynyslas, there was really no alternative but to build the line along its northern shore. This involved the construction of several short tunnels to take the line around the town of Aberdovey and an alignment close to the shore, the track bed protected from the incursions of the sea with retaining walls. The line met the existing route from Aberystwyth to Machynlleth at a remote location surrounded by water and salt marshes which was originally called Glandovey Junction. It did not receive its current and more familiar name of Dovey Junction until 1904.

An equally challenging route had to be forged to take the line the four miles north from Llwyngwril to the shore of the Mawddach estuary. A ledge on which to lay the track had to be carved in the cliffs over 80 feet above the shore at Friog. This was the scene of two alarmingly similar fatal accidents in 1883 and 1933 when trains ran into boulders and debris that had fallen onto the track from the steep hillside above. In both instances the locomotives derailed and fell to the shore below killing their crews. Fortunately, on both occasions the coaches remained on the track otherwise the death toll could have been much

worse. In response to the second accident, the Great Western Railway built a reinforced concrete avalanche shelter to deflect any future rock falls onto the shore below. This is a feature rare in Britain, one more commonly associated with Alpine railways.

From Friog the line dropped down to sea level on a gradient which was 1 in 55 at its steepest point. It passed through Fairbourne where the CR opened a station in June 1899 at the site of what had been, in 1865, a temporary terminus called Barmouth Ferry which closed when the Barmouth Bridge was completed. The bridge across the Mawddach estuary was the greatest challenge faced in the construction of this line. It consisted of 113 timber trestles and three metal spans at the Barmouth end, one of which could be opened to allow the passage of ships up the estuary. It would be a further two years before it was completed, trains finally reaching Barmouth in September 1867. The footpath across the bridge was there from the outset and has been delighting visitors to the area ever since. One nineteenth-century tourist guide extolled its virtues by saying, 'there is not such a promenade pier in Europe.'

Whilst the bridge was being built, work continued on the final stretch of the line to Portmadoc and Pwllheli. It stayed close to the coast, skirting Harlech Castle and crossing the Traeth Bach on a wooden trestle bridge at Penrhyndeudraeth. The line approached Portmadoc across land reclaimed from the sea by the great embankment built by the Festiniog Railway in the 1830s. It was further inland than the narrow gauge line which meant that the station was located on the northern edge of town and there was no access to the harbour. The line through to Pwllheli opened in October 1867 and made a junction with another new railway which had opened just a month earlier. This was the 26-mile-long route which ran from Menai Bridge, on the Chester and Holyhead line near Bangor, through Caernarvon to a junction with the coast line at Afon Wen. Like Dovey Junction and Barmouth Junction, this was

yet another location created by the railway. There was no town or village there. Afon Wen, which was located on the edge of the sea about four miles from Pwllheli, owed its existence to the need to have a place where passengers and goods could be transferred from one line to another. The line to Caernarvon was acquired in 1869 by the London & North Western Railway who, by this time, also owned the Chester to Holyhead line.

The line from Dovey Junction to Pwllheli was 54 miles long. By the time it had been completed, the Aberystwyth & Welch Coast Railway had become part of a much bigger company. In June 1864 the Cambrian Railways (it was always the plural form which was used) was formed with the amalgamation of the four small companies who had built the line through mid Wales and its connection onwards to the Shrewsbury to Crewe line at Whitchurch; the Llanidloes & Newtown, Oswestry & Newtown, Newtown & Machynlleth and the Oswestry, Ellesmere & Whitchurch. The A&WCR amalgamated with the CR in 1865.

This new Welsh company, whose headquarters were in England, at Oswestry in Shropshire, had a main line 96 miles long from Aberystwyth to Whitchurch. The coastal route was always worked as a branch off this main line and is still largely seen as such to this day.

The CR was never very prosperous and indeed it went into bankruptcy in 1868 and again in 1884, though it managed to retain its independence on both occasions. When, in 1923, Britain's many independent railway companies were merged at government insistence into four large groups, the Cambrian became part of an enlarged Great Western Railway. However, the Afon Wen to Caernarvon branch, owned by the L&NWR became a component of what was, at the time, probably the largest railway company in the world – the newly formed London, Midland & Scottish Railway. This remote outpost still remained a junction between two different companies.

The GWR made some improvements to the line. A number of additional halts were opened. Three of these, Gogarth, Abertafol and Penhelig, were on the stretch between Dovey Junction and Aberdovey alone. Some services from Pwllheli now ran through to Chester and Birkenhead via the Dee Valley line which joined the coastal route at Barmouth Junction and GWR locomotives began to replace older CR engines on the trains. Perhaps the most famous innovation introduced by the GWR was the line's very own named train, the *Cambrian Coast Express*. This first appeared in the timetables in 1927. For most of its existence it ran during the summer on Fridays and Saturdays only, though British Railways operated the train every weekday from the late 1950s. The *Cambrian Coast Express* ran from Paddington to Birmingham Snow Hill and then on to Wolverhampton where there was a change of engines. It took the Abbey Foregate Curve to bypass Shrewsbury and stopped at the main stations as far as Machynlleth where it divided, one portion going to Aberystwyth and the other to Pwllheli. Timings from 1963 show the train leaving Paddington at 11.10am and reaching

Aberystwyth and Pwllheli at 6.56 and 7.30pm respectively. With the run down of services on the former Cambrian lines and the GWR main line north of Birmingham, the through service was transferred to London Euston but even this had gone by the early 1990s.

One other significant traffic flow which developed in the 1950s was that generated by the Butlins Holiday Camp at Penychain near Pwllheli. A halt had been opened there in 1933 and work on a holiday camp started in the same decade. The incomplete camp became a Royal Navy training establishment called *HMS Glendower* during the Second World War but opened its doors as a holiday camp for the first time in 1947. This led to the GWR doubling the track from there to Afon Wen, extending the original platform and building a second, one both of which could now accommodate ten coach trains. During the high season special trains ran to the camp on Saturdays from a range of destinations. Those from the North of England used the Bangor to Afon Wen or the Dee Valley lines. Services also ran from South Wales. In the summer of 1959, there was a through train from Swansea running via Lampeter and Aberystwyth with advertised connections from Newport and Cardiff. The journey time from Cardiff using the through service from Swansea to Penychain was a few minutes under nine hours!

The Cambrian Coast Line was not among those slated for closure in the infamous Beeching Report of 1963 but the routes which joined it, the lines from Barmouth Junction to Ruabon and Afon Wen to Caernarfon were. However, its future was still far from secure. In 1967 it became apparent that it was not to be included in government plans for the future national network, and closure proposals were announced in 1971. There was a predictable outcry both locally and from railway supporters around the country which led to the line being reprieved in 1974. What survived was very much a basic railway. The only stations which retained staff were Pwllheli, Barmouth and Towyn, with tickets at most stations and halts henceforth issued by conductor/guards on the trains. The line lost most of its remaining freight traffic in the 1970s and then in 1980 it was found that a species of marine worm was burrowing into the wooden piers of the Barmouth Bridge. The immediate effect of this was that diesel locomotives were banned from the line and the remaining freight traffic, from the explosives factory at Penrhyndeudraeth, was lost. For a time, the activities of the naval shipworm, or *teredo navalis* to give it its scientific name, once again called the future of the line into question. But fortunately British Rail repaired the bridge and locomotives were once again able to run on the line.

The first generation diesel multiple units which had replaced steam trains on the route were themselves phased out in the 1980s. New 150 class units were introduced along with a marketing drive to promote the unquestionably splendid scenic attractions of the route. Unfortunately, seat and window spacing on the new trains, which were designed to cram as many commuters in as possible, meant that one's view of the scenery was sometimes interrupted or blocked by the side of the carriage. In the first decade of the new millennium, the former Cambrian lines were used to trial in Britain a new European train control system called the European Rail Traffic Management System, an electronic system which eliminates the need for conventional trackside signals. After extensive testing ERTMS was used to control all trains on the line from the Spring of 2011. Its use has not been without the odd technical problem but at least the investment in this state of the art technology bodes well for the long term future of the route.

Most of the stations and halts on the coast line are still served by trains today, unlike the Shrewsbury to Aberystwyth line on which only the major stations have survived. Trains usually divide at Machynlleth with one portion going to Aberystwyth and the other serving the Pwllheli

line. Additional passing places have been added to the main line with a view to introducing a much needed hourly service between Shrewsbury and Aberystwyth, though whether this will improve the frequency of trains on the coast line remains to be seen as the cutbacks of previous decades have eliminated many of the places where trains can cross on the single line. A modern diesel train may not have the romance of the steam hauled *Cambrian Coast Express* but nothing can detract from the enduring majesty of the scenery on the coast line and it is fair to say that, with the value of railways belatedly being rediscovered, it is hard to see how any further threats to this magnificent route would ever be taken seriously.

MACHYNLLETH

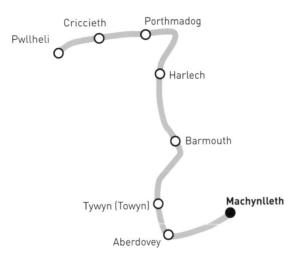

Pwllheli
Criccieth
Porthmadog
Harlech
Barmouth
Tywyn (Towyn)
Machynlleth
Aberdovey

Our journey along the Cambrian Coast line begins, as have so many others for countless decades, at Machynlleth. There is no better way to start than with a look at the line's very own named train, the *Cambrian Coast Express*, seen arriving at the station on 11th July 1962 hauled by *Manor* class 4-6-0 No 7823 *Hook Norton Manor*.

After a short run of about four miles, trains came to Dovey Junction where the Coast Line diverged from the former Cambrian Railways main line to Aberystwyth. Set in the marshes at the edge of the Dovey Estuary, the remote Dovey Junction was a creation of the railway. There was no road access to the site which, until the reorganisation of local government in Wales in 1974, spread out into three counties; Cardiganshire, Montgomeryshire and Merionethshire which met at this point. In this view taken on 10th May 1965, No 7812 *Erlestoke Manor* is leaving the station's island platform with the 6.00pm Aberystwyth to Shrewsbury service. Coast Line trains used the other face of this platform. No 7812 was one of a number of *Manors* which survived the end of steam and is still regularly seen in action in Shropshire on the now preserved Severn Valley branch of the former Great Western Railway between Bridgnorth and Kidderminster.

Looking in the opposite direction to the previous picture, towards Machynlleth, on 18th May 1963, BR Standard Class 4 2-6-4 tank No 80070 arrives at Dovey Junction with a stopping service to Pwllheli, passing a fine gantry of GWR lower quadrant signals. From the late 1950s onwards, the new BR Standard classes began to appear on the line which had hitherto been almost exclusively the domain of GWR designs.

After leaving the Junction, trains crossed the River Dovey and then hugged the north bank of the estuary most of the way to the first station at Aberdovey about six miles distant. This part of the line was virtually level and the GWR opened three halts on this section in the 1920s and 30s; Gogarth, Abertafol and Penhelig. This view of a two coach local service bound for Barmouth approaching Gogarth Halt on 13th June 1964 hauled by ex-GWR 0-6-0 No 3208, shows how close the line was to the coast for most of this stretch.

ABERDOVEY

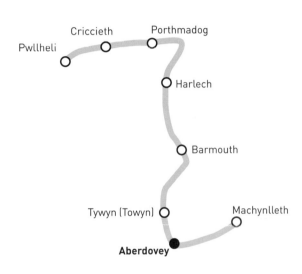

Pwllheli — Criccieth — Porthmadog
Harlech
Barmouth
Tywyn (Towyn) — **Aberdovey** — Machynlleth

This view of Aberdovey station was taken on 9th May 1967 looking towards Dovey Junction. The main station buildings were on the Up platform and the small signalbox which contained just 20 levers is to the right of the picture on the opposite side. The canopy on the Up platform has an interesting history. In an early example of recycling, when Pwllheli station was relocated nearer to the town centre in the early twentieth century, the canopy from the original 1867 station was installed at Aberdovey. It was on the move again 70 years later when it was dismantled and re-erected at Llanuwchllyn, the terminus of Rheilffordd Llyn Tegid/Bala Lake Railway, where it continues to perform its valuable function of sheltering prospective passengers from the Welsh rain.

In the 1960s, an unidentified pair of BR Standard class 4 4-6-0s, storm out of Aberdovey with a long passenger train bound for Pwllheli.

Aberdovey was briefly a terminus in the 1860s before the section to Dovey Junction opened and the promoters of the line had high hopes that Aberdovey could be developed as a port. A short steeply graded branch was built down to the harbour and, though some sailings did run to Ireland, by the 1880s coastal shipping was all that served the harbour. The branch, which remained in situ until the 1960s, was also known as the Sand Siding. In this undated but probably 1920s view, a former CR 0-6-0 is seen at Aberdovey Harbour. The locomotive was one of a class of three built at the Vulcan Foundry at Newtown le Willows in Lancashire in 1895 as CR No 78 and renumbered 881 by the GWR at grouping.

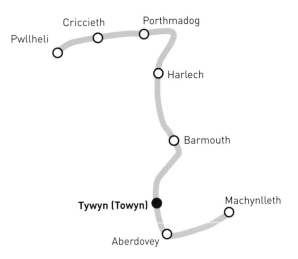

TOWYN

Towyn, the next station, was three and a half miles of mostly level track from Aberdovey. Trains approaching Towyn pass Wharf Station, the terminus of the Talylynn Railway. The siding once used to load slate brought down by the narrow gauge line is to the left of the train and narrow gauge wagons can be seen in the TR sidings parallel to the Coast Line as BR Standard Class 4 No 75021 approaches Towyn with a stopping train for Pwllheli in the summer of 1966.

Pwllheli

Criccieth

Porthmadog

Harlech

Barmouth

Tywyn (Towyn)

Machynlleth

Aberdovey

Looking in the other direction towards the station, ex-GWR 2-6-0 No 6375 leaves Towyn with the 1.55pm stopping passenger service from Barmouth to Dovey Junction on 10th July 1962.

The Pwllheli portion of the *Cambrian Coast Express* arrives at Towyn on 10th September 1958 hauled by ex-GWR 2-6-2 tank No 4575. The signalman on the raised platform beside his box has just exchanged tokens with the fireman. On single lines such as this the token was the authority to proceed onto the next section of track. It could only be released when the signal boxes at either end of the section, which were linked electronically, had confirmed to each other that the section ahead was clear. This was supposedly a fail-safe system but human error involving the issuing of a token at Abermule, a station on the single line between Welshpool and Newtown, on 26th January 1921, allowed two trains to crash head-on resulting in 17 fatalities, the worst accident by far in the history of the Cambrian Railways.

Between Towyn and the next station, Torfanau, the line followed the sea shore and in an effort to protect the trackbed from erosion and inundations, large boulders to form a defence against incursions from the sea were placed beside the rails, as can be seen in this view taken on 16th May 1952. The train from Machynlleth to Barmouth is hauled by ex-GWR 4-4-0 No 9012 which once carried the name *Earl of Eldon*. This was an interesting design dating from the 1930s but looking much older. It was a hybrid using the frames and boilers of two earlier types of 4-4-0s, the *Bulldog* and the *Duke* classes, hence the nickname applied to these locos, that of *Dukedogs*. The GWR, which was remarkably deferential to the landed gentry and named hundreds of their locomotives after their stately homes, planned to use the names of suitably titled aristocrats on the *Dukedogs*. It is alleged that some of those honoured took umbrage that their names were appearing on such humble machines and they were quickly transferred to new *Castle* class main line engines. Whatever the truth of that tale, these light yet powerful locomotives were a mainstay of services on the Coast Line in GWR days.

Generations of railway staff have required constant vigilance to keep this part of the line safe for traffic. Bridges and structures such as these were maintained by the GWR Oswestry Division's Bridge Department which was based at Caersws. These men were responsible for looking after most of the GWR and latterly BR network in mid Wales as far south as Brecon as well as the former Cambrian lines to Aberystwyth and Pwllheli. On

25th September 1960, a former LMS steam crane is being used to place massive boulders to strengthen the sea defences near Towyn.

Beyond Tonfanau station, which did not have a passing loop but once had a siding serving a nearby quarry and extensive sidings dealing with traffic to a large army camp close to the station, the line begins to climb for the first time since leaving Dovey Junction. On 7th May 1952, ex-GWR 2-6-2 tank No 4549 approaches Tonfanau with a passenger train from Barmouth to Machynlleth.

Beyond Llwyngwril, the Coast Line climbs steadily towards one of its most spectacular features, the cliffs at Friog. The track is perched on a narrow ledge between the hills and the sea which is here being negotiated by a northbound goods train beheaded by BR Standard Class 2 2-6-0 No. 78005.

The potentially hazardous position of the railway at this point is perhaps best appreciated in this view from the beach where the locomotive in the 1883 accident ended up. Taken on 27th September 1961, this shows an unidentified former GWR 2251 class 0-6-0 heading south with a local train for Machynlleth.

In the space of about a mile, on gradients as steep as 1 in 55, the line dropped down from the cliffs at Friog to sea level at Fairbourne which had briefly been the terminus of the line in the 1860s when Barmouth Bridge was under construction. On 14th September 1964, ex-GWR 0-6-0 No 3208 is seen at the station on a three coach stopping train. There was no passing loop at Fairbourne, the points in the foreground lead to a short siding.

After the gradients leading to Friog, the track was level to Barmouth Junction where the line from Ruabon met the Coast Line. The station was renamed Morfa Mawddach by British Railways in June 1960 but with the closure of the line to Ruabon in 1965, Morfa Mawddach lost its importance as an interchange between the two routes. Today it is a shadow of its former self, a one platform request stop on the Coast Line, its fine station buildings replaced by the sort of shelter usually seen at bus stops. However, traces of its abandoned platforms can still be found and it is the ideal starting point for a walk across the Barmouth Bridge on what is surely one of the most spectacular footpaths in the whole of the British Isles. On 13th June 1956, the signal man is exchanging tokens with the fireman of *Dukedog* No 9028 as it arrives at Barmouth Junction with a Coast Line service. The tracks leading to Llangollen and Ruabon are to the right of the locomotive.

Even though the romance of the age of steam has long gone, a journey across the Barmouth Bridge is still a memorable railway experience. In this 1960s view, an unidentified BR Standard class 2 2-6-0 at the head of a four coach local passenger train trundles off the southern end of the bridge and heads towards Morfa Mawddach. Most of the bridge consists of 113 wooden trestles. Their infestation by wood-loving marine worms in the 1980s almost led to the closure of the line.

On the 9th May 1952, at the other end of the Barmouth Bridge, ex-GWR 2-6-0 No 5334 brings a service from Ruabon off the bridge. The nearest of the metal spans at the northern end was originally capable of being opened to allow shipping to pass through the bridge and continue up the estuary.

BARMOUTH

Pwllheli
Criccieth
Porthmadog
Harlech
Barmouth
Tywyn (Towyn)
Machynlleth
Aberdovey

Barmouth station was often a busy place. On 10th June 1954, ex-GWR *Dukedog* class 4-4-0 No 9000 leaving with the 2.00pm Barmouth to Dovey Junction train passes *Manor* class 4-6-0 No 7800 *Torquay Manor* which will haul the next service, the 2.35pm Barmouth to Chester train.

The previous summer, No 7800 *Torquay Manor*, the first member of the class to be built by the GWR in 1938, prepares to leave at Barmouth with a stopping service to Wrexham.

There were two halts between Barmouth and the next station Dyffryn; Llanaber and Talybont. These were under the control of the Station Master at Barmouth and, unlike many of the halts on the line which were opened by the GWR, these two dated from Cambrian Railways days. On 4th September 1964 BR Standard Class 3 2-6-2 tank No 82003 is approaching Llanaber with a stopping train. Neither Llanaber or Talybont had road access, both were reached by footpaths from nearby minor roads.

Dyffryn Ardudwy has had several names since it opened in the 1860s. At first it was called simply Dyffryn but presumably to avoid confusion with another GWR station called Dyffryn in the Rhondda Valley, it was renamed Dyffryn-on-Sea after grouping. It assumed its current name under yet further new owners in 1948. It had a passing loop and was fully signaled from this original CR signalbox situated, along with the main station buildings, on the Up platform.

HARLECH

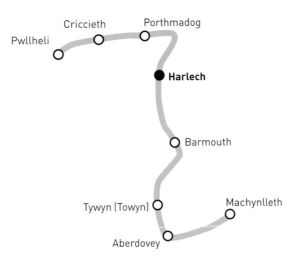

There can be no mistaking this location. The railway line and the station at Harlech lay on flat land under the shadow of the famous castle to which the GWR paid due homage by naming one of the first batch of its superb *Castle* class express locomotives introduced in 1923, No 4095 *Harlech Castle*. The size and weight of those machines meant they were not allowed west of Shrewsbury so the chance of a photo opportunity featuring the two could never be realised. On 30th June 1959, BR Standard Class 4 4-6-0 No 75020 leaves Harlech with a four coach stopping train for Dovey Junction.

This unusual view of the station, taken from high above on the ramparts of the castle shows the superb strategic location of the fortress which dominated the landscape for miles around. For the record, the activity far below at the station on 22nd August 1952 is of an ex LMS 2-6-0 leaving with a train for Pwllheli. It has just crossed a southbound goods train hauled by an ex-GWR 2251 class 0-6-0 which is still standing at the station.

Nine years later in April 1961, the goods from Pwllheli was still in charge of an ex-GWR 2251 class 0-6-0, on this occasion No 2255, which simmers at Harlech station waiting to cross a northbound passenger service.

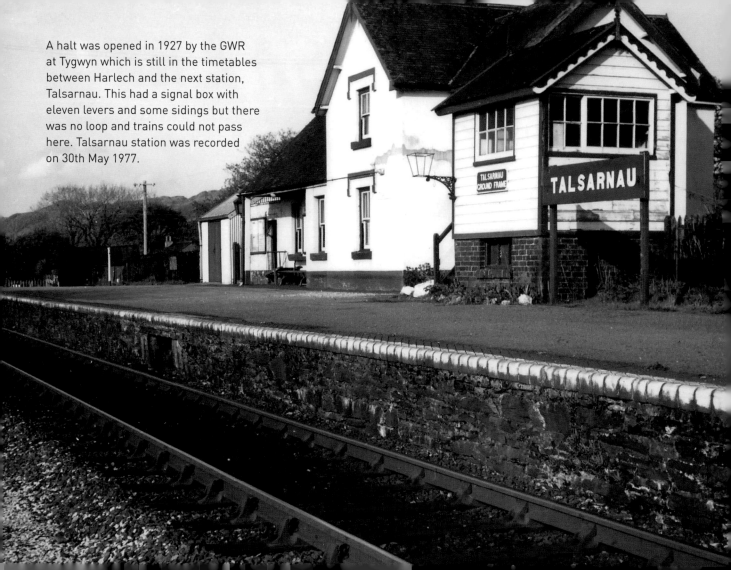

A halt was opened in 1927 by the GWR at Tygwyn which is still in the timetables between Harlech and the next station, Talsarnau. This had a signal box with eleven levers and some sidings but there was no loop and trains could not pass here. Talsarnau station was recorded on 30th May 1977.

After passing another GWR-era halt which opened in November 1935 at Llandecwyn, trains approached Penrhyndeudraeth. Part of the village can be seen in the background in this undated pre-grouping view of a CR 4-4-0 on a passenger train crossing Pont Brwyt which carries the railway over an inlet of the estuary. In the winter of 2013, work on rebuilding the adjacent road bridge led to the destabilisation of the railway bridge and disrupted train services on this part of the Coast Line for many months.

PORTMADOC

Portmadoc (Porthmadog today) was always an important station on the Coast Line and remains so to this day. It had an engine shed which, as late as 1947, at the end of the GWR era, had an allocation of nine locomotives. By the mid-1960s steam was rapidly being replaced by diesel multiple units on passenger services. A four car formation waits to form the 3.42pm stopping service to Barmouth on 12th May 1966. This train was run only in term time and was largely for the benefit of scholars.

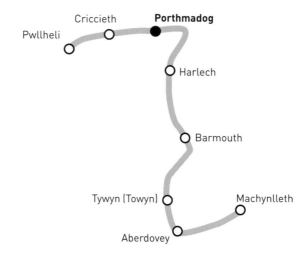

Pwllheli
Criccieth
Porthmadog
Harlech
Barmouth
Tywyn (Towyn)
Machynlleth
Aberdovey

A few years earlier in 1960, when steam was still king, ex-GWR 0-6-0 No 2244 leaves Portmadoc station with a short goods train.

Three miles beyond Portmadoc, trains came to Black Rock Halt. This was the first halt opened by the GWR, entering the timetables in September 1923. Its purpose was to allow holiday-makers to visit the nearby Black Rock Sands and it remained open until the 1970s. On 24th September 1948, ex-GWR 2-6-2 tank No 4518 prepares to stop at the halt. Even though British Railways had been in existence since 1st January 1948, the locomotive still has its number painted on the buffer beam in GWR style and has not yet acquired a metal smokebox number plate which were fitted by BR to all its locomotives.

Criccieth, 46 miles from Dovey Junction, was another important holiday destination. On 22nd June 1953, brand new BR Standard Class 2 2-6-0 No 78000 which had only been built earlier that year, the first of a new class of 65 locomotives, approaches the station with a service to Pwllheli.

CRICCIETH

In the summer of 1938, GWR 0-6-0 No 2298 pauses at Criccieth station with a Down stopping service. When the track work along the Coast Line was being rationalised in the 1960s the passing loop was removed and trains can no longer cross here.

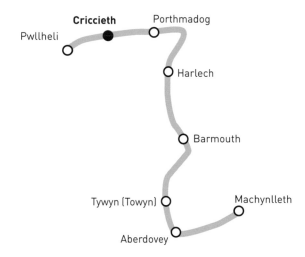

Pwllheli
Criccieth
Porthmadog
Harlech
Barmouth
Tywyn (Towyn)
Machynlleth
Aberdovey

On 26th May 1954, the 10.30am Barmouth to Pwllheli goods train arrives at Criccieth in charge of ex-GWR 2-6-2 tank No 5533. The arrival of this train would be followed by some shunting to transfer wagons to the substantial goods shed to the left of the picture over the unusual and complicated layout of points and crossovers which were in place here. At this time, before the dominance of the lorry, small towns such as Criccieth would have most of their requirements delivered by local goods trains such as this.

The next station after Criccieth was Afon Wen, a substantial junction set on the edge of the sea in the middle of nowhere. It was the point of interchange between the Coast Line and the former LNWR/LMS line which ran from Bangor via Caernarvon. This line opened before the Coast Line and for a very short time in September and October 1867, trains from Bangor ran through as far as Penrhyndeudraeth. This ended when the Afon Wen to Pwllheli section was completed. On 18th July 1946, an LMS 2-6-2 tank No 42 arrives at Afon Wen with a train from Bangor.

This scene, recorded at Afon Wen station in the summer of 1932, shows both its substantial station buildings and lengthy platforms. The GWR train on this Coast Line service is something of a period piece. The locomotive is a *Barnum* class 2-4-0, one of 20 dating from 1889, the last of which was withdrawn in 1938. The first two carriages have clerestories (raised sections in the centre of the roof), a feature which was popular in the late nineteenth and early twentieth centuries designed to provide better headroom, ventilation and room to hang lamps.

A mile beyond Afon Wen, the GWR opened a halt at Penychain in July 1933. Building work on a holiday camp began here in the late 1930s but before it opened war was declared and it became a naval establishment for the duration called *HMS Glendower*. In 1947 the site finally opened as a holiday camp run by Butlins and from then into the early 1960s attracted thousands of holiday makers, the vast majority of whom came by train. The line between Penychain and Afon Wen was doubled and the original halt with a single short platform was transformed into a large station with two lengthy platforms with bi-directional working which could accommodate ten coach trains needed to cater for the large numbers of passengers who came during the summer months. Penychain was treated as a station for those few months of the summer peak each

year but reverted to the status of an unstaffed halt for the rest of the year. On 23rd June 1965, a train from Pwllheli hauled by BR Standard Class 2 2-6-0 No 78007 arrives at the station.

There was one final halt at Abererch on the final three mile section of the Coast Line between Penychain and Pwllheli. As it was the line's terminus, Pwllheli needed an engine shed. This was always considered an out-station or a sub-shed of Machynlleth, some 57 miles distant. The original single road wooden building was replaced as late as 1959, when the writing was already on the wall for steam, by the new two road steel framed building seen here in the year it opened. In the foreground is ex-GWR 2251 class 0-6-0 No 2286. The smokebox of the engine seen on the line behind it is that of *Dukedog* No 9017, the only survivor of its class which is now preserved on the Bluebell Railway in Sussex.

In the last year of the GWR's long innings (it was originally promoted in 1833) a pair of GWR locomotives leave Pwllheli with a train for Dovey Junction on 3rd April 1947. The leading or pilot locomotive is *Dukedog* No 9004 whilst the train engine is 2-6-2 tank No 5507.

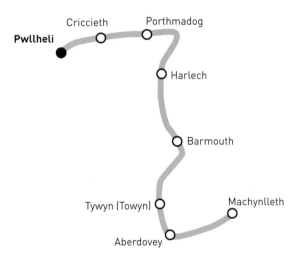

Pwllheli

Criccieth

Porthmadog

Harlech

Barmouth

Tywyn (Towyn)

Machynlleth

Aberdovey

Our pictorial journey along the Cambrian Coast Line began at Machynlleth with a view of *Manor* class No 7823 *Hook Norton Manor* at the head of the route's most famous train, the *Cambrian Coast Express*. There is a certain symmetry in ending with the same locomotive seen here simmering at the buffer stops at Pwllheli having just arrived with a stopping passenger on 6th August 1963.

CREDITS

Lost Lines of Wales – Cambrian Coast Line published by Graffeg March 2016
© Copyright Graffeg 2016
ISBN 9781909823204
Author Tom Ferris

Graffeg Limited, 24 Stradey Park Business Centre, Mwrwg Road, Llangennech, Llanelli, Carmarthenshire SA14 8YP Wales UK
Tel 01554 824000 www.graffeg.com

Graffeg are hereby identified as the authors of this work in accordance with section 77 of the Copyrights, Designs and Patents Act 1988.

A CIP Catalogue record for this book is available from the British Library.

Photo credits

© Kidderminster Railway Museum: pages 11, 16, 17, 20, 21, 22, 25, 26, 27, 28, 29, 30, 31, 33, 34, 35, 36, 39, 40, 42, 44, 45, 49, 50, 51, 53, 54, 55, 56, 58, 59, 60, 62.
© R. F. Roberts/SLS Collection: cover image and pages 12, 14, 18, 24, 43, 47.
© P. Ward/SLS Collection: page 38.

Other titles in this series:

Lost Lines of Wales
Brecon to Newport
ISBN 9781909823181

Lost Lines of Wales
Aberystwyth to Carmarthen
ISBN 9781909823198

Lost Lines of Wales
Ruabon to Barmouth
ISBN 9781909823174